What is the Dog Doing?

By Cindy Olejar

2014

One of the intentions when reading this book is to practice using present tense singular verbs to say what the dog is doing in the photo. See if you can come up with other verbs that are not in the book too. Be creative!

Cindy Olejar lives in Seattle, WA.
To contact the author email
cindyolejar@yahoo.com

What is the dog doing?

Murphy

The dog **is hiding** behind the shed.

The dog **is peeking** out from behind the shed.

What is the dog doing?

Max

The dog **is chewing** on his toy.

The dog **is lying** in the grass.

What is the dog doing?

Maizy

The dog **is riding** in the cart.

What is the dog doing?

Alley

The dog **is looking** out the window.

The dog **is resting** her head on the couch.

What is the dog doing?

Barkley

The dog **is drinking** water.

The dog **is standing** at the water bowl.

What is the dog doing?

Beau

The dog **is looking** at the cat in the window.

What is the dog doing?

Linus

The dog **is fetching** the ball in the water.

The dog **is having** fun in the lake.

What is the dog doing?

Josephine

The dog **is riding** in the car.

The dog **is gazing** out the window.

What is the dog doing?

Leon

The dog **is burrowing** in his blanket.

The dog **is keeping** warm in his bed.

What is the dog doing?

Ziggy

The dog **is lying** on his back.

The dog **is relaxing** on his back.

What is the dog doing?

Penny

The black dog **is chewing** on a stick.

The dog **is hanging** out with three little pugs.

What is the dog doing?

Red

The dog **is jogging** at the park.

The dog **is carrying** the ball.

What is the dog doing?

Stewie

The dog **is resting**.

The dog **is lying** on the ground.

What is the dog doing?

Oscar

The dog **is swimming** in the water.

The dog **is exercising**.

What is the dog doing?

Murphy

The dog **is sitting**.

The dog **is smiling**.

What is the dog doing?

Nico

The dog **is balancing** on the log.

The dog **is** dirty.

What is the dog doing?

Cory

The dog **is shaking** his body back and forth.

The dog **is wearing** a harness.

What is the dog doing?

Murphy

The dog **is running** on the beach.

The dog **is** at the beach.

What is the dog doing?

Otis

The dog **is sitting** on his hind legs.

What is the dog doing?

Murphy

The dog **is digging** in the dirt.

The dog **is making** a hole in the dirt.

What is the dog doing?

Mugsy

The dog **is resting** in the hole.

The dog **is relaxing**.

What is the dog doing?

Murphy

The dog **is visiting** the dinosaur park.

What is the dog doing?

Buddy

The dog **is standing** on the grass.

What is the dog doing?

Molly

The dog **is lying** in the mud puddle.

The dog **is soaking** in the water.

What is the dog doing?

Petunia

The dog **is posing** for a picture.

The dog **is sitting** very still.

What is the dog doing?

Murphy

The dog **is carrying** a toy.

The dog **is** at the park.

What is the dog doing?

Red

The dog **is wading** in the water.

The dog **is cooling** off in the water.

What is the dog doing?

Cory

The dog **is standing** in the way of the broom.

What is the dog doing?

Stewie

The dog **is fetching** the ball.

The dog **is playing** in the snow.

What is the dog doing?

Max

The dog **is resting** on the porch.

The dog **is looking** out.

What is the dog doing?

Gigi

The dog is _____.

The dog is _____.

What is the dog doing?

Murphy

The dog is _____.

The dog is _____.

What is the dog doing?

Bodhi

The dog is _____.

The dog _____.

What is the dog doing?

Murphy

The dog is _____.

The dog _____.

What is the dog doing?

Josephine

The dog _____.

The dog _____.

What is the dog doing?

Max

The dog _____.

The dog _____.

THE END

Made in the USA
Charleston, SC
05 October 2014